KILLING SUMMER

SARAH BROWNING

SIBLING RIVALRY PRESS
DISTURB/ENRAPTURE
LITTLE ROCK, ARKANSAS

Killing Summer
Copyright © 2017 by Sarah Browning

Cover art, detail from *They Hate Us for Our Freedom*
 by Esther Iverem, fabric and mixed media, 48Hx64L.
Author photograph by Jill Norton Photography.
Cover design by Seth Pennington.

All rights reserved. No part of this book may be reproduced or republished without written consent from the publisher, except by reviewers who may quote brief excerpts in connection with a review in a newspaper, magazine, or electronic publication; nor may any part of this book be reproduced, stored in a retrieval system, or transmitted in any form, or by any means be recorded without written consent of the publisher.

Sibling Rivalry Press, LLC
PO Box 26147
Little Rock, AR 72221

info@siblingrivalrypress.com

www.siblingrivalrypress.com

ISBN: 978-1-943977-40-6

Library of Congress Control No. 2017943798

This title is housed permanently in the Rare Books and Special Collections Vault of the Library of Congress.

First Sibling Rivalry Press Edition, September 2017
Second Sibling Rivalry Press Edition, May 2019

KILLING SUMMER

Contents

        1.

15	Petworth, Early Evening
16	After Poetry and Photographs in an Anacostia Gallery
17	Langston Hughes Joins the Merchant Marine, 1923
18	Headline: *Six Killed in Raid*
19	The Fort
20	Rembrandt Workshop in the District
21	Harry
22	In My Bus Station Locker
23	Girl Talks Back
24	I'm not homeless, my son fell asleep
25	Reading Dante's *Inferno*, or The Anniversary of Hurricane Katrina
26	Gas
28	Killing Summer

        2.

33	Girls in Red on Page One
34	File Room, University Health Clinic
35	For Dangerfield Newby, Freedman
36	Burning and Splendor
37	Hard-Headed Woman
38	When the sun returns
39	In Guantanamo
40	Yemenis Question U.S. Drone Strategy
42	The Color Clang and Jangle
43	Governor Bradford Watches the Indians *Fall Into Lamentable Condition*, 1633

45	Coming on Red
46	Aching to Graduate
47	Kissing Girls
48	Going to See the Caravaggios
50	This Is the Poem

3.

55	Drinking as a Political Act
57	More and More
58	A Brief History of the Number Two
60	Kissing Boys
61	Fasting
62	The Great Books, or All Theory and No Practice
63	Photo of a woman with nipples and a cigarette
64	Report Back: Torino in April
65	In the Dream He Was Light
66	After the Lightning Storm
67	The Walton Mountain Museum
69	Hot Priests
70	One White Expanse

4.

75	London Holds Its Breath
77	The Blueberry Seasons
78	Greeting
79	I go for days
80	The Blue Devil
81	Amputees
82	Foreclosure
83	Titian's *San Cristoforo*
84	Rainy April Fools' Day in Italy
86	Farm Country, Western Massachusetts

87	Kin
88	Cawing Down the Airwaves
89	A Small Portion
92	Flag of No Walls

Dedicated to the memory of my mother, Ann Hutt Browning, and my grandmother, Marjorie Hutt.

For Ben, always.

1

Petworth, Early Evening

A man is stabbing women in my neighborhood.
Most poor people in my city are Black

and because of the warnings of 400 years
I assume the man stabbing women

is Black. Walking home, I pass
a young Black man on the sidewalk.

When I first spotted him I did not
cross the street, though I thought to.

As we pass he reaches into his pocket
and I feel fear, how white I am.

From his pocket he pulls
a phone. Calls his girlfriend or grandma

or buddy up the street, his job, his pastor,
his boyfriend, his AA sponsor. I don't want

to be afraid of my neighbors, walking home
from the Metro in the clear light of evening.

I want to tear history from my throat.

My son is in his room texting his friends.
It is June in the 21st century.

After Poetry and Photographs in an Anacostia Gallery

Girls, age 10, read poetry. We applaud wildly,
read our own poems, drink lemonade, eat cheese

in the muggy Washington night, as portraits
of the neighborhood stare down

from the gallery walls. Driving home
across the river, on the off-ramp I spot him

and just swerve: a man, there, teetering.
So thin. Quickly he is gone behind me.

Yes and no on the same evening —
the world comes to us like this.

At the end of the reception a young man
appears beside me with a paper cup.

I have not seen his swollen face before.
I fill his cup with lemonade.

No one asks him to leave.
He eats some cheese and some more.

Langston Hughes Joins
the Merchant Marine, 1923

Langston drops all his books except *Leaves of Grass*
into New York Harbor, so that

the two poets lie down together in the cramped
hold of the ship, wrapped in the hammock

of language — song of themselves spooning
in the middle of the ocean. Uncle Walt whispers

to Langston out on the blue, cajoles, welcomes him —
stretching vocal cords, straining body: ship, men, hunger.

Langston touches and is touched, ship-sheen of the other,
skin the question, skin the answer. No land, but music.

Headline: *Six Killed in Raid*

> *Six American soldiers and an Iraqi interpreter*
> *killed in booby-trapped house.*
> — Fourth paragraph of a *Washington Post* story

Seven.

The Iraqi interpreter lent
his tongue, teeth, the tender
upper ridges of his mouth
to the Americans.

I used to believe
the secret of seven
was its spike and splendor.

We won't know
his name, his burying
place, the tea he drank,
his daughter, the shoes he wore.

The Fort

He is small, not a man.
Not even a young man.
He is a boy.
He knocks one sister down
in the tall grass.

I'm going to have you
he tells the girl lying silent
at his feet.
Have you and then burn you.

In the fort the sisters
built two blocks from home.

Go get matches
he tells the other sister.
Boulder chair, boulder TV.
Chipped plate from home.

Bent spoon.
Run and go get matches.
He is small. Not a man.
The sisters silent,
the younger runs toward

home as if toward matches,
calls at last to the men
on the porch. But she left
her sister in the tall grasses.
She left her there, in the grass.

Rembrandt Workshop in the District
National Gallery of Art

Stingy with the light,
this maker—only two faces:

Christ, who lives forever dead
in the painting, lowered by the arm

of a man hidden in a dark corner.
But here, the sun strikes the mother,

her grief well lit
for tourists and students

who stare at her—
the mother on the front page

of the Metro section, well lit
in grief for a son who

*dressed like a girl, changed his name
to Aisha* and died in a car,

shot, along with *that other one*,
two blocks from home.

Harry

It's here I was born.
Except those seven years
at the state hospital,
I always did live right
here at 42 Cedar Lane.

My sister Annie moves about,
tells me nothing about her world:
Harry, have you tied up the tomatoes?
I'll be making green tomato and watermelon
pickle this year, same as last.

Seven years at the state hospital
don't tell me where else
I ought to be.
Cured, it says, in a book in town.
Anyone can look it up.

The honeysuckle's growing wilder,
I suppose I could say.
The glider needs greasing.
The mints Annie's making go down
smooth or hot,

depends which one you choose.
The cows are quiet on the hillside —
flies and bees their noisy neighbors,
Black-Eyed Susans, Queen Anne's Lace
their showy sisters.

In My Bus Station Locker
1983

Road maps — the old and gray
and the crispy new ones. Cigarettes,
a picture of a 20-year-old in a '64 Chevy,
a certain openness, another kind of shut,
leg warmers, categories of butch girls
and some femmes. Two photos
of naked hippies at the hot springs —
more than enough want to carpet
the state of Washington, especially all
those intervening years, especially
the Columbia River at its mouth,
Cape Disappointment Lighthouse
flashing; a quart of Rainier Beer,
the fizz going out, the bus station
crowded or quiet. Buses leaving town.

Girl Talks Back
After a photograph by Sally Mann

I don't give a fuck
if you take my picture
like this. Everyone says

I'm pretty. Gold, they
call it, all this hair.
Yes, it's a real cigarette.

I smoke when I feel
like it, see, and where-
ever. What are you doing,

hanging around playgrounds
taking pictures? My mama
says to watch out for pervs

in playgrounds. But you just
like to look, right? I know
that's what you like.

I'm not homeless, my son fell asleep

Sitting propped
against the storefront,
I try yelling it
at the people staring
their clenched stares.
The pavement is cold
against my ass, the child
so hard asleep against me
I can yell and not wake him.
One woman smiles.
Another just keeps looking,
forgetting to smoke.
Most look — quick —
and look away.
I watch all of them passing.
I could just turn
my palm to the sky,
hold out my empty hand
to everyone I see.

Reading Dante's *Inferno*, or
The Anniversary of Hurricane Katrina

In Hell's lowest circle, the Betrayers stand
half-submerged in icy waste, and frozen.

Archbishop Ruggieri locked Ugolino in a tower
with his four small sons and there they starved, the boys

calling to Ugolino for aid he could not give. Now
Ruggieri may not even cry, eyes so crusted with ice.

The children died first. The father watched.

Gas

After the great snow of 2016, my car sits
locked in icy drifts a week, green fossil
of the oil age preserved in graying amber.

I relearn the art of walking, of reading
pocket paperbacks on the bus, which uses
this same stuff, this gas, to bear us through

the snow-narrowed streets of Washington, DC—
Capital of Exxon, Capital City of Shell;
still we are two dozen here driving one tank.

Once the rains come and the weather gang
shakes their collective heads as the mercury
rises to 60 degrees, my car is free to roam again

the Precincts of BP, the Republic of Sunoco.
I'll drive my car to the climate change rally.
I'll drive it to the poetry reading that protests

war in Iraq, that denounces repression in Syria,
that stands in solidarity with poets locked up
in Saudi Arabia. My car gives me that much

freedom and power, plus music to soothe me
and a phone charger to keep me connected
to my comrades in struggle. My car glides

smoothly in and out of gear, builds my self-
esteem as I parallel park perfectly each day
in tight spots on the hill where we dwell.

The weather scares me. The wars enrage me.
The poets, silenced by the despots, break my heart.
But my car needs me. My car is nothing

without me. My car and I are one. I pledged
my allegiance long ago—an American century
ago—to my beautiful, necessary, beloved car.

Killing Summer

The *Washington Post*, Section B, Local Briefs:
another boy dead, and another —
Across town.
Down the block.
In the alley.
In his car.
A few feet from a middle school.
At a bus shelter.
Dead at the scene.
Pronounced dead at the hospital.
Motive unknown.
Suspects unknown.

*

City of split heads, city of gun shops threatening,
city of playing the dozens across the steaming streets.

Streets of rain and fast anger, streets
of whistling, streets of mourning.

Mourning silence of lamp post shrines,
Sunday dinners cooking slowly in stewpots.

Stewpots of greens and fatback, all manner of potatoes,
pork that tumbles begging from the bone.

*

The dead young men lie in the city morgue, keeping
company with their dead brothers. It is Saturday.

July in DC, killing summer.
Shake out the newspaper.
Shake death from the bus shelter.

What city are we?
How do we call ourselves neighbors?

2

Girls in Red on Page One

Still clotted with sleep I retrieve
the paper from the porch.

So often children on page one
are laughing, learning new rhythms

of Brazilian Capoeira—tipped
in red sashes one against another—

or rolling Easter eggs
on the White House lawn.

In that slow-drawn moment
of waking, as I scan the *Post*

in the hallway, I think these girls too
are in that open red joy only children know.

But no—it's a Baghdad
city block, school girls torn—

What idea, what god,
what future

what temple, what word
is worth these girls?

Their faces open
not laughing but gashed, open.

File Room, University Health Clinic

My mother's Assistant Director
so it's nepotism, but I work hard,
making new covers for sick workers'
fat files, tattered and sad. Shelving.
The women whose days are filled
with the file room will have nothing
to complain about in me. Not like
the director's son who, last year,
didn't do nothing. I take my daily lunch
into the sun—lemon yogurt, sunflower
seeds, V8—sit tucked on the grass
to read from the AP English Summer List:
Sons & Lovers. Catalogue of miseries.
I'm 16 but at Chances R they serve me beer.
I throw peanut shells to the floor
with tipsy abandon. *Kiss me now*
I want to say to my friend Don.
I want daring. I have D.H. Lawrence
in my long bones, file folders in my fingers,
a summer of Turgenev and Hardy to tangle
all my beery knots.

For Dangerfield Newby, Freedman

This is for Dangerfield Newby, lying quiet amid the muskets
and white men in the fire house in Harper's Ferry, waiting.
This is for Dangerfield Newby, and all those men whose families
worked some other farm, waiting to be sold, waiting for the carts
and whips to take them south. This is for Dangerfield Newby
who would not wait, who chose the gun and John Brown
and the town we know with its high vise of cliffs and beauty.

We do not know Dangerfield Newby.
So this is for him, who loved and hated and could no longer wait
and so chose the gun. For Dangerfield Newby, who was the first
man dragged from the fire house in 1859 and shot
through the throat. The volunteers beat his still body in the dust,
slipped their knives from sheaths at their waists
and sliced the offending ears from his broken body.

This is for the ears of Dangerfield Newby.
They had heard possibility—to lie again beside
a woman whose name we do not know,
a woman who could not choose.
This is for the ears of Dangerfield Newby
that heard an echo from those blue hills,
from the shallow whisperings of the two rivers.
Lying in the separate pockets of white men—
on two tables at the tavern—even on display
in the separate homes of white men—the ears
of Dangerfield Newby each heard a single word: freedom.

Burning and Splendor

> *To make injustice the only*
> *measure of our attention is to praise the Devil.*
> — Jack Gilbert

I'm hot, Dan's sister writes in his notebook. Then, *I'm Cuban*,
rejoicing in her own wanton beauty wired up in the ICU,

glad and bountiful, the tube in her throat refusing silence.
Dan's sister dances in the *ruthless furnace of this world*,

glad for Dan's arrival, though it frightens her that he's come
so far, glad for Dan's notebook he carries everywhere to record

the burning and splendor of this world. Jack Gilbert died yesterday.
Sorrow everywhere. And suffering. But let us not praise the Devil.

Let us bring the notebook to Dan's sister. Let us declaim
that in the furnace of this world she is Cuban. She is hot.

Hard-Headed Woman

I'd heard Cat Stevens singing
so I was ready to believe
a man lived who was looking
for a hard-headed woman.
But the smart boy editors
on the high school newspaper
in 1979 were looking instead for
Candy Chatham, who
climbed into their laps
in the fluorescent night
of the student center lounge.
I tried turning away
with a look I hoped was
hard-headed, finished typing
my story on the new exhibit
of lithographs in the school library.
My coeditor Charlie shrugged.
What could he do, Candy perched
and vivacious on his uncertain lap?
Cat Stevens got religion, changed
his name to Yusuf Islam.
I got the ache of his voice turning
scratchy on the turntable
late into the dorm room night.

When the sun returns

it is hallelujah time,
the swallows tracing an arc
of praise just off our balcony,
the mountains snow-sparkling
in gratitude.

Here is our real life—
a handful of possible peonies
from the market—
the life we always intended,
swallow life threading
the city air with
our weaving joy.

Are we this simple, then,
to sing all day—country songs,
old hymns, camp tunes?

We even believe
the swallows, keeping time.

In Guantanamo

A man composes a poem
pressing his thumbnail
into the white permanence

of his Styrofoam cup—
Arabic script of praise song,
of lament, circling the cup,

cup of our disdain. Hail the
cup, singing its squeaky dirge
in the land of our castoffs.

Hail the poet's nail, thumb,
muscle, and hail his nerve.

Yemenis Question U.S. Drone Strategy

According to the Long War Journal, *at least 116 people were killed in U.S. airstrikes in Yemen last year.*
— Washington Post, *February 9, 2014*

Yemen's Interior Ministry apologized

> *Thy mother's name is ominous to children*

the cousins were innocent... it was "their fate" to die

> *From forth the kennel of thy womb hath crept*
> *A hellhound that doth hunt us all to death*

every effort to minimize civilian casualties

> *Put in their hands thy bruising irons of wrath*

people give them intelligence —

> *Plots have I laid, inductions dangerous,*
> *By drunken prophecies, libels, and dreams,*

and then it turns out that the U.S. targeted a political rival

> *To set my brother Clarence and the king*
> *In deadly hate the one against the other*

Every time they kill an innocent person

> *Reap the harvest of perpetual peace*
> *By this one bloody trial of sharp war*

they motivate the families to join al-Qaeda

Long mayst thou live to wail thy children's death

The Color Clang and Jangle

James Lee Woodard, cleared of the 1980 murder of his girlfriend ... incarcerated longer than any other wrongfully convicted US inmate cleared by DNA testing.
— Washington Post, *2008*

In the picture, Woodard is captured
from below, so we see more
of the wild pattern, streaked beauty
of his wide tie than we do of his face.
We can't say if it's satisfaction
or the great expanse of city street
that must be before him. The purple
shirt strains with his raised arms,
holding high the white hands
of his smiling attorneys on either side.

The story doesn't give the girlfriend's
name so we will call her Cheryl.
*Dear Cheryl, 27 years I wake
each morning with your blood.
I imagine the knife.
Did you whisper my name?*

Here on the courtyard steps
the color sun
the color purple shirt
the color Cheryl
the color 27 years
the color president
the color America
the color time.

Governor Bradford Watches the Indians
Fall Into Lamentable Condition, 1633

In the swamp spring
of Plymouth, Essex,
Narragansett Bay, they miss
the rush of mackerel
into nets — for the Indians
lie dying on their hard mats,
the mackerel make their way
unhindered and the Indians go hungry.

The pox loves hunger, seeks it
like the hunter, quiet
in the woods that no one
burned last year, too busy
were the Indians being Fearful
to Behold, their skin flaying
and *cleaving by reason thereof
to the mats they lie on.*

The pox runs up to the next
village and the next, traded
the way the Indians of the south
used to trade corn to the Indians
of the north, they tell us, for animal skins —
so there is no warmth this winter
and the Indians *lie down to die
like rotten sheep.*

Which is how the Lord
cleared the land,
bleached it pure, the *pox breaking
and mattering and running
one into another*,
seeking brethren in the body
of these lamentable creatures —
all of a gore blood.

Coming on Red

Tell me, is it true the sky was red:
blood, heart, of course, and shame,
war, rare birds in the yard

And rags, truck, fire, spark, what I know
of you, you of me, rage, night—

how it winks at want
how it comes on red

Aching to Graduate

I lie in the grass, reading
The Heart of the Matter,
hope the knot of boys nearby
is watching me. I will happily
betray the suicidal colonial cop Scobie,
sweating out his life in an unnamed African land,
for a real-live boy in the sun.

Ants travel my leg.
I hear the boys laughing.
I try to look relaxed,
like the other sunbathing girls
sprinkled on the lawns around campus.
I try to look like I am enjoying my book,
but not too much, like my hands would fit
just as nicely around a boy's tight waist.

Trading insults, aching to graduate,
the boys take off their shirts.
One runs off to sail a perfect frisbee
winging back to the others,
who rise together to the challenge.
I pick up *The Heart of the Matter*,
flick the ants from my white calf,
go back inside.

Kissing Girls

Barbara Muldoon won't let me
unbutton her paisley blouse—
tangled here in my narrow
boarding school dorm room bed—
though we've been wild
with drunken kisses for nearly an hour.

She stops my hand and stops it
again. Her mouth tastes of Molson Gold
and mine of another kind of gold, just
now learning to hold the sweet smoke
in my lungs long enough to start loving
my own unwieldy body, the press
of something sweet between my thighs.

Barbara sighs, our tongues touch
again—wrap each other in a new warmth
then withdraw, then touch again.
We are learning how talented the tongue can be.
I want to use its new skill on Barbara's brown
nipples I've spotted coming out of the shower—
I can almost taste them in her beery breath.

The Grateful Dead plays quietly through
the walls—*Friend of the Devil* boy sound
I'd never heard 'til I came to this strange place—
and I don't know the rules here, now,
whether I'll want to keep on kissing girls.

Going to See the Caravaggios
Brera Museum, Milan

The pretty, pouty boys
at the center of *The Musicians* —
on loan from the Met — are thick-lipped,
grumpy, sick of this sport of sitting.

They've sat already for *Sick Bacchus*
and *Boy With a Basket of Fruit*, hanging
here as well, on loan
from Rome's Villa Borghese.

One will be *Medusa*, too —
so feminine that mouth, and the snakes
androgynous enough for any critic.
Just one Caravaggio

in Brera's permanent collection:
The Supper at Emmaus, Christ
and his followers — as usual
some backs, some bread.

But I turn back to the pretty boys,
drawn by men's desire for one another,
the boys' full lips parted as a woman's
would not be in 1602,

their willingness on display.
The boys are done with pretending
to play the lute. They're ready
for the real thing: the tumble,

the cock, painted lips full open.
Their necks are stiff from turning
to watch the artist who cannot
stop watching them.

This Is the Poem

I am on the Parkway with Fred, driving home
from Baltimore to DC. We've been to a packed

and riotous tribute to Ms. Lucille Clifton
at the public library. How we start talking

about history and my slave-owning forebears
and poetry I don't remember, but that's how it is

with Fred—we talk about these things.
I tell Fred I've been trying and failing

to find my way into the head
of my great-grandmother or anyone else

who owned other people, trying to imagine.
Fred says, Well, maybe that's not the poem.

Maybe this is the poem—you and I,
a Black man and a white woman,

crossing state lines below the Mason-Dixon Line.
The traffic stalls for late-night repairs

and we stop, between these two cities.
We are friends in a car.

And how could the Black men mutilated
and beaten and thrown in rivers

for just this—talking with a white woman,
crossing state lines, riding in a car—

not come and congregate with Fred and me
as we sit quietly a moment?

Construction lights flash in our eyes.
I wonder about the white women—

where are they in this story?
How could they bear

what had been done in their names?
Was there ever one who said no?

3

Drinking as a Political Act

The way my Virginia daddy made them,
mint juleps were a sacrament:

He folded ice cubes inside a clean
tea towel then pulverized them
with a wooden mallet that wasn't used
for any other purpose,

picked mint he'd grown and tended
in a strip of rich black earth that
hugged the south side of our house
on the south side of Chicago.

My Virginia daddy'd been with
Dr. King on the bridge in Selma, so
I didn't know 'til I was a middle-aged
white woman that some Black folks did not

share my view of the julep as a rare
and noble drink, but, rather, knew it
for what it was, plantation-born: ice
crushed by the strong arms of their

ancestors, sweetened with the blood
of others sold south to cut the cane.

I don't mean we forget my Virginia forebears
who sat out on their wide porches and sipped
the minty coolness of the labors of people
they took to be their property. I don't mean

forgiveness, even. I mean, let me make you
a sweet, ass-kicking julep. Let's raise a glass
to those who unmade that hideous life,

who, with their hard, truth-telling love,
keep unmaking it each day.

More and More

The trick is not to be so satisfied
           with more and more of everything
that feeds a grievous hunger.
                      — Bruce Weigl

I can't seem to account for my heart—
enormous crow on the telephone pole
cawing three times across the hidden
part of the neighborhood—alleys,
garages, cars on blocks, spilled
chicken bones and diapers.
The church bells are starting up.
In the dream, an old love appeared
and called to me. I couldn't reach him,
even the dream a cliché, each door
a false beginning.

The church bells play "America the Beautiful."
The mourning dove echoes a big wind
in the oak tree. Somewhere, as ever, a siren—
no Sunday morning peace. I outstare
the neighbor's cat. I think there is no god
lolling in the clouds, enjoying
the praise. So I beg forgiveness
of the cat, the overgrown garden.
There will always be two stories.
Mine will be the bad dream,
cliché, tut-tut.

A Brief History of the Number Two

*For Navenka Gritz, mother of David Gritz,
killed at Hebrew University, July 31, 2002*

I can hardly stand to look
but the mother looks and looks—
the same photo again and again
on bookshelves, bedside table,
kitchen windowsill, dresser—

listens to the voice of her son
in the old cassette tapes
he made—Sibelius,
Led Zeppelin, Brahms—
while working in her studio,

winding the thread tight.
Each finished piece
is for him, he lives
in this yellow bead, this thread
circling the bead, its sheen
is the son, its route on the board
the body the mother washed,
each hair she stroked
in the morning, waking him.

I want to wake him, her son,
and send the other boy—
the bomber—home
to his own mother,
whose knees one day

will give out,
whose fingers will cramp.

I want to tell the bomber
to choose to live.

Kissing Boys

My tits feel nothing
when Joe Templeton
lifts my peasant blouse
to touch

I do this out of respect
he says
which hardly
helps

Joe's lips
are warm—
damp oatmeal

I push back
but nothing works
Finally Adele Gray

dorm head to smart girls
opens the basement door
and saves me

Really, Sarah
Adele shakes her head—
The grownups
don't want me

to do what
other girls do

Fasting

Each year on Oxfam Day we fasted,
our meal money going for world hunger.
We knew it was symbolic.

Oxfam buttons pinned to our awkward
chests, we gazed with drawn looks
at the low New England hills.

Our teachers knew on this day not to press us
on Aeschylus. Tomorrow we'd be back to
our eager selves, cursing Agamemnon's slaughter

of his sweet Iphigenia, amazed that the gods could
truly ask for such a thing, a daughter. All we knew
of sacrifice was the pink Fish Newburg and pale

Brussels sprouts we skipped at dinner.
We didn't believe in fate, destiny, the inevitable.
But here was Agamemnon dead in his bath,

his son Orestes set on his own path to murder.
At night, in our rooms, we inhaled the yellow scent
of popcorn, heard the rollicking cascade of the popper

down the hall. We listened as each kernel
exploded, but stayed true to the gods' demands,
went to bed early for once, cleansed for one more year.

The Great Books, or All Theory and No Practice

We read *Emma* but didn't need an older Mr. Knightley
to teach us to be kind. The older men already liked us
and we were kind—geeks and misfit boys sat
with us in the dining hall and followed us to chapel.

We read *King Lear* but those girls only wanted their fathers' love
or something called Land. We already had our fathers,
admiring us from afar, our As and AP classes.
And all the land we could want stretched out around us

in farms and football fields and the small hills of New England.
We read *The Wife of Bath* but none of us seemed destined
to marry an old guy and sleep with an innocent scholar.
We were the innocent scholars, all theory and no practice.

We read *The Lysistrata* but we'd had no sex to withhold.
We couldn't believe we'd ever have such power.
At night one month we all read *Hot Summer Chicks*,
a teacher falling on her pupil when she accidentally spots his size.

We didn't care about size. We would have done with
kisses, vague gropings in the woods, a book to tell us
how to love the boy and the world, the father and the land.
The book of longing we're each of us still writing.

Photo of a woman with nipples and a cigarette

Is she baring or bared?

The flame is a nipple. I shake

when I see it. The nipples wing

the woman into me. They hum

in the kitchen late at night.

I am red wine in the glass.

I am a crumpled napkin

on the table. I am the flame.

I am traveling to the dark lips.

The flame will soon expire.

No, it won't.

Report Back: Torino in April

If they ask what it was like,
say it was gray so many days
we dreamed the color chart of gray—
Pearl, Opal, Imperial Half-Tone Gray—
none of which is on display
in the shiny tourist brochure.

Think Italy, think sun: Yellow!
Gold! Siena!—a whole color
named for that imagined
glowing city to the south.

But here in Torino, tucked up against
the Alps—we know they ring the city
but if you ask us we can only gesture
helplessly to the north and to the west—
here, we are connoisseurs of precipitation:
drizzle, mist, downpour, my English
mother's favorite word: mizzle.
Hail twice now in April. Games cancelled.
Trips delayed. Laundry drying
for days on indoor racks, tired
soggy sweat socks of gray.

Travelogue of gray, pastry shop
of gray, full moon of gray.
Today: gray.
Tomorrow: we promise
to stop arguing, to wallow,
luxuriate, fall in love.

In the Dream He Was Light

The beard softened him
to milk in her throat
like her tongue that one time

slowly tasting him, like the way
he smiled for once,
choosing the sun.

In the dream he was soft
and laughing and wondered at the way
people from our past become us,

they are what we are —
our soft ticking,
the sheets we lie down in

next to our husbands
and our wives.
The sun grows in some people,

plants itself
and grows — in dreams,
on storm drains, even on stages.

After the Lightning Storm

The fridge shudders
silent, lights blinker

out, the fan slows and
slows its whirring. Time

ticks by without language
or sputter. She wonders

at her cold and starry heart,
welcomes burn and

burr-hedge, sedge-weed
and whistle cricket.

A sleek rusty newt
slips from under the stairs.

Come, country heat.
Come, stump and swing,

sting of pine tar and
timpani—wear me down.

The Walton Mountain Museum
Schuyler, Virginia

The board game, John Boy's earnest face
huge in the foreground. The Christmas
album, all seven children, Ma, Pa, Grandma,
Grandpa, holly garlands. Lunch box. Thermos.
Three *TV Guide* covers. Model truck, very rare.
Dolls, each in its window-box package, each
in its overalls: Jim Bob, Jason, Ben. I had forgotten
Jason, forgotten Ben. Forgotten even Mary Ellen —
those faces come back to me, John Boy's first sex
on Walton Mountain, his sunburnt butt. And I almost
blush for my child self, how much I remember that episode,
John Boy, writing poems, gazing out at the Virginia night.
Good night, Ma. Good night, Pa. Good night, John Boy.
My friend Alison mocked me for crying at *The Waltons*,
the rising melody, swelling Hollywood chords, parents
who loved each other and only argued over the big questions —
sex, racism, one child's coveting the simple toy of another —
resolved in one hour, including commercial breaks,
didn't rage over 45 years. Who wouldn't cry? The hugs,
tender glances, Earl Hamner, Jr. weaving my parallel
childhood from his own nostalgia, while sipping brandy
in his Hollywood den. Is it fair, Earl, all these even-handed adults,
all this love flooding back into the last scene? No one goes to bed
resentful or full of racist hate or wanting to flee to Hollywood,
seven children in love with the mountain, one another, Grandpa —
Will Geer, working again, freed from the Black List
and happy for it, I'm sure, everyone getting rich, the show
at #1 for years, despite opening against *Flip Wilson*

and *The Mod Squad*—so that now, Earl, the people still
come to Schuyler, where the soapstone plant closed
generations ago and the population shrank to 600.
Your youth's on display: in the yearbook—
the only boy in a graduating class with 16 girls—
do you remember, Earl, or has Richard Thomas'
sunburnt butt crowded out your own? And what's an authentic
childhood anyway: the hours I spent each week in fear
that my father's fist might slam the dining room table,
hours spent dreading my mother's pinched and silent look,
or the one hour I spent each week with Mary Ellen, Elizabeth,
Jason, whom I'd forgotten, Ben, whom I'd forgotten—
one hour each week when the music rose, violins soared,
I could cry, and the grownups took care of things.

Hot Priests

The calendar hangs on every souvenir stall in Rome,
beside Audrey Hepburn and Gregory Peck
circling Piazza Venezia on a Vespa.

January's a simple seminarian from Akron, but March
smolders in his love of the Lord. A sullen Fabio, his long
black hair is brilliantined, a two-day growth on his chin.

I check out the live ones, who stride purposefully
in their gray-black-brown-white robes across
the cobbled alleyways and frantic boulevards of the city.

Young, buff, from all the wondering Christian world, they
come to Rome. They study, pray, live in beloved community.
Once I start looking I cannot stop: peke-faced or angelic.

Senegalese. Korean. Filipino. Italian. Their robes swish —
they *swish* — with their devotion. I am so agog I quit reading
the guidebook — how the Titus Arch celebrates Rome's

pacification of the Judaic people — to gaze at their hard backs.
I can't help thinking of all that Catholic flesh in the news.
And the calendar pin-ups, are they models or the real thing:

beefcake, true and holy?

One White Expanse

*Stuck in the slime they say: We chose to be sad
In the sweet air enlivened by the sun,
And our hearts smoldered with a sullen smoke.*
— Dante's Inferno

Today—no sun, the sky one white expanse.

Put on the shoes of sadness.

Tie the laces. Walk through

the sad Italian city. Laughing

ragazzi with their cigarettes: sad.

Barista stacking cups in the dishwasher

all day: sad. Flirting cheese and salami

guy pushing two mozzarella balls

when I ask for one: sad. His sweet

seductive smile even. Sicilian clementines

themselves, waxy orange in the basket

on the kitchen table. Arduous accumulation

of days—churches, Baroque masterpieces,

agnolotti in sage butter sauce, ornate elevator

with red vinyl seat: all sad.

Dante's 741 pages:

Centuries of sad.

What sweet air, what sun?

4

London Holds Its Breath
for Ann Hutt Browning

For months the shelters are homes for fear,
families tired and waiting forever
together underground.

Your cold cucumber sandwiches
grow soggy in your palms.
How familiar is the thermos,

its dulled shine in the darkness
and the damp of the underground.
You listen to the whiz and whir

of the Blitz raging above you.
You bury your long face in the crook
of your mother's arm.

But no air raid sirens tonight, calling
high and low across the neighborhood.
The dark is observed — the city holds its breath.

Here's an engine in its overnight home
flashing blue and hot orange
in the quiet railroad yard.

The silence is only dull
like the engine's roar.
You hold your mother's hand

and step across the tracks.

Tonight you are on your way
and America is promised.

Your mother is dreaming of the sailing
you will make together. She tells
you tales of New York, big cars

crossing the vast cornfield, the ocean
dancing on the other side, California,
the golden hillsides, your new home.

The Blueberry Seasons
for Ben

In December, I dream of August, the drive
along the lake, past trailers and 4-H camps,
wineries and cabins, you in the back seat,
telling stories of cousins and rope swings.
We are the only ones who wanted to come.

Long past when I think we should have arrived,
I spot the sign: Glenhaven Farm.
The farmer gives us buckets
and we head up the rows together,
then you rush off ahead. Every year

I am astonished by the plenty,
the sheer purple weight as the berries
fall to our greedy, tender fingers.
We will take them home, our sacks
heavy with the sun,

your grandma will make pie
and everyone will admire our handiwork.
I can't stop admiring you, how you run
like that, bring your bucket now to show me.
A few seasons, a few seasons.

Greeting

New white folks
in the neighborhood

don't know to greet
a stranger on the street.

They don't mean
to be rude.

How long will it last, then —
How ya doing?

Eye to open eye.

I go for days

I go for days forgetting these pictures —
bare brown bodies stained and curled
on cement floors or cowering in a corner,
the dog's teeth more real than the man's terror,

which we know from history will likely
deaden into numbness in the man, then turn,
grow menacing as an improvised
explosive device. I go for days forgetting.

In war, in the aftermath of war
bridges collapse into rivers, sense
into nonsense, bodies into meat —
offal on the slaughterhouse floor.

Another man, imprisoned here nine years —
shackled days, electric chair sizzling
in anticipation. The state was mistaken
it seems, pays the man money.

He struggles to rebuild the bridge
of his life collapsed into those years.
He is a big man who tells his story
every day and every day he cries.

I don't remember his name
from the newspaper. I don't
know the names of the Iraqi men
in the pictures I go for days forgetting.

The Blue Devil
Dome of the Baptistry, Florence

Imagine the scaffolding 100 feet
closer to God, craftsmen placing
the tiny tesserae in five shades
of blue for the horns, for the ears,

adding brown and a touch
of yellow for the serpenty heads
thrusting from each ear, then
a ghostly kind of white:

sorrowing human bodies
caught in the serpents' mouths.
To the glory of God, to His glory,
this Satan—ravenous setting

of blue square upon blue square,
lifetime upon lifetime. Next the belly
with its concentric whorls, the arms

muscular, strong enough to hold
two more of the tortured
in his curling fingers. *Help me
oh Lord*, thinks the grandson

watching his father and his grandfather
working side by side 100 feet
in the air. *Make me worthy
of Thy Last Judgment.*

Amputees
Washington, DC

In our city we see them sometimes,

out for the day with a girlfriend:

new-fangled leg still learning to walk

in a style we call natural. Metal joint

exposed by shorts that flaunt

the terrific other leg, too.

Arms intact, one hand holds

an ice cream cone, the other

the girlfriend's hand, as they stroll

jerky across the plaza to the fountain

where they join the other couples—

also bloodied though we may not

know it—trying not to stare.

Foreclosure

Blind eyes to the street now.
Forgotten jump rope in the yard —

pink plastic handles turning
dusty in the summer heat.

Was it wrong to hope, to dig
a hole for the lilac bush now

struggling through its first season?
She hates herself when she does it,

but still she does: Walk the long way
to the bus so she can water the roots.

She can't seem to let it die.

Titian's *San Cristoforo*
Doge's Palace, Venice, 1523

The saint's massive muscled arms —
arms for the forge, for fighting, for tending

and laboring — reach toward heaven, toward the baby god
on his shoulder, who himself gestures toward heaven,

gripping the saint's shoulders with his fat feet,

so the painting is filled by the saint and his
huge bare thigh — Venice a tiny sketch of city at his feet.

Titian loved this man.

Rainy April Fools' Day in Italy

The daffodils I bought at the market
are two-toned trumpets declaring desire,
its thump and grind: empty.
I've got half a mind to tell it off—
all of spring—and another half to turn
the anger inward. The rain drips.

Somebody promises fulfillment
but the same someone is stuck
in the circle of Hell Dante reserves
for flatterers: *Don't you think
that I deserve it?*
asks the customer, and the harlot replies
You do, you're marvelous,
and so condemns herself.

Who's the lying son of a bitch in that story—
the borrower, the lender, Dante's whole underground
world of Florentine rivals writhing in Hell
for aligning with the wrong side?
Money grubbers and wasters. Gluttons.
Heretics and skeptics. Tyrants. Sexual perverts.
Suicides. Plunderers. Deeper still, pimps.
And then, even lower, *flatterers*. Not as damned
as futurologists and hypocrites but well
below the murderers and squanderers.

I can't imagine anyone's out there
flattering this rain, the clock's angry tick.

I'm not. I've got my own pain to think about,
how it takes up residence all day.
What's the difference now: rain or sparkling spring.
We're all made of one thing
and the same is true of its opposite.
Crawl around inside your despair. Tap on its walls.
Test its floorboards. Will it hold your weight?

Farm Country, Western Massachusetts

October and sloppy ruts threaten
the delicate underbelly of your car.

You want to slough off steel
and walk away, let stone walls,

faded tobacco barns, choking
Farmall tractors take you,

to be forgiven by chipmunks.

You want this myth of field mice,
cider-sweet air, legend of pumpkins,

cows pretending to be serene:
you want to learn from their slow cud

how to stand in one corner
of one pasture and chew.

Kin

The peonies are perfect freaks —
white heads too ponderous
for their slender bodies
they bow almost to the ground —
where, suddenly, a large rat,
the city announcing itself.

This week I tried to tame
my own wild reaching
and failed. I've no talent
for restraint. How can I
teach it to the honey-
suckle, English ivy, riotous
ground cover, hydrangea
that threatens the tea rose
with its excess?

Sister Rat, tell me what
comes next: will we capture
you, poison you, starve you
and all your cousins, here
in my yard with the praying
peonies, the rose run raggedy,
grasses gone to seed?

Cawing Down the Airwaves

Hate pulls up a bar stool to watch the All-Star Game
in city neighborhoods and on country roads all over the land.
Hate roots for the American League.
Hate roots for the National League.
Hate roots for the Dominicans and the Cubans
on TV screens above bars up and down the land.

Hate takes to the sky at dusk, cawing down the airwaves,
circling over suburban lawns and swimming pools,
just now trimmed and skimmed by the uncles of the children
at the border, their fathers and cousins.

Hate hollers at its own children, as they climb the steps
of the bus taking them off to summer camp, lest they forget
to hate the aunties of the children at the border, the aunties
even now sweeping the cabins and preparing
potato salad and burgers for Hate's children.

Hate is languid one minute, heated the next.
Hate applies sunscreen and reaches for a thriller,
tilts back its lawn chair and sips its Coke.

The children at the border look sweet enough.
It's not personal, Hate allows. It's just—you know—
Hate got here first.

A Small Portion

> *For the men of Washington, DC, incarcerated at Rivers*
> *Correctional Facility, four hours from their families.*

Their pens inclined — some for the first time —
to the page, the men, two days, longing
for the soft and fuzzy heads of their children,
for Sunday games of pitty-pat in the backyard
while their own Mamas bake cakes through
kitchen back doors.

Leonard's Mama: *Get your raggedy ass*
to school. Rodney's arms pocked
with the needle's remembrancers, pink
scars everywhere on the pecan tan of his skin —
pecan tan a phrase I praise for its assonance,
its surprise, the sweet hard *A* sounds.
The men laugh, it's nothing new to them,
pecan tan, common praise words for a fine
Black woman. Then I laugh too, point
at my own arm, how white one woman can be.

Today I am learning Mike's grin
when he stands to read what he has written.
I'm no poet, he says, then reads a poem.
You could warm the bottles of a thousand babies
on that smile, a smile to give us new definitions
of the word *sweet*. Where is the image-simile-
metaphor (tools I try to give them)
for that smile of Mike's? A smile to make
the mourners at the dignified funeral
stomp for the sheer pleasure of the life now lost.

I hadn't expected beauty—charm, hustle, maybe,
but not sheer beauty—shy Jermaine in the corner
a high school football star who's just made
the big touchdown; John, who recites
his full name each time he stands to read
what he has written, then
Washington, DC, Northwest—
his locator, even here in the Tidewater flats
of North Carolina, BBQ country, cotton country.

*

On the TV commercial for Prison Break
the men are vicious. We can tell by the
fast editing, shaved heads, tattoos

(Jay, the goofiest of the men at Rivers,
the jokingest, teasingest, has tattoos
of snakes and crosses and the whole world
up the length of both arms), by the clanging
music and for the first time I think of the Mamas
who see that ad, who don't get to the clicker
in time to change the channel.

*

Here in my backyard in Petworth,
a squirrel flings itself from the roof
of my neighbor's car park
to a spindly branch on the oak tree.
Next door, Gary's cooking the city's best
jerk chicken for the baby shower for the baby

who came too soon. The friends,
the cousins and uncles, will eat rice
and peas, smile at the chicken-spice
and celebrate a new life, a baby boy.
The squirrels will pitch in their own
chattering hosannas. I try to imagine
the ten men at Rivers today: playing
cards, writing their daughters, watching
Prison Break. Let there be sun, but not too much.
Let one small syllable of hope, or even a few—
a new haiku of hope—sprout from the hand-
out I printed off the web at the hotel at night,
unprepared as I was for their hunger for form.
That might do for one day—for any of us—
a small portion, improbably rich.

Flag of No Walls

On the border with Mexico
we call it a fence, as if
to lean on its top, chat
with those neighbors
to the south, trade rakes,
trade gossip. Call it a fence,
call it a gate, call it good—
still, Nogales, Arizona,
Nogales, Sonora: trench,
ground sensors, infrared
night-vision scopes.

In Palestine, the land's already
been taken—families on one side,
orange groves on the other.
Ours is a culture of many walls
the Saudi poet writes in her email.

Young people sat on the Berlin Wall
and waved the flag of no walls.

Here's to the flag that waves
like that, for bricks
that go home in tourist
luggage, for the Saudi poet
and her sisters, for touch.

Flag of men waiting
for work in the morning chill

of the 7-11 parking lot,
flag of nannies pushing
strollers to the park
for fellowship and swings,
flag of the women
who spend each day
changing the soiled sheets
of their new country.

I want the flag of talking,
of sitting on the disintegrating
wall and gabbing, gossiping,
negotiating, waving that flag
of no walls. That flag.

Notes

"Burning and Splendor" is for Dan Vera and in memory of José "Joe" Gouveia. Quotes from Jack Gilbert are from his poem, "A Brief for the Defense," in *Collected Poems* (Knopf, 2012).

"Yemenis Question U.S. Drone Strategy" alternates lines from the *Washington Post* story of the title, February 9, 2014, and *Richard III*, by William Shakespeare.

Quotes in "Governor Bradford Watches the Indians *Fall Into Lamentable Condition*, 1633" are from William Bradford's *Of Plimouth Plantation*, a journal written between 1630 and 1651.

The quote from Bruce Weigl in "More and More" is from "The Burning Oil Rises Through the Wick," found in *Declension in the Village of Chung Luong* (Ausable Press, 2006).

Quotes from Dante's *Inferno* in "One White Expanse" and "Rainy April Fool's Day in Italy" are from *The Divine Comedy* by Dante Alighieri, translated by C.H. Sisson (Oxford University Press, 2008).

"This is the Poem" is for Fred Joiner.

"The Fort" is for Katie Browning.

"Girls in Red on Page One" is for Persis Karim, Beau Beausoleil, Shatha Almutawa, Helen Frederick, Nikki Brugnoli Whipkey, and all the writers, artists, and activists of Al-Mutanabbi Street Starts Here.

"A Small Portion" is additionally for Carol Fennelly and Hope House DC, a program dedicated to helping incarcerated Washington, DC, fathers stay connected to their children. Learn more at www.hopehouse.org.

Acknowledgments

Many thanks to the editors of the following journals and anthologies where some of these poems first appeared, sometimes in earlier versions:

Al-Mutanabbi Street Starts Here, Beloit Poetry Journal, Beltway Poetry Quarterly, Big Bridge, Boxcar Review, Broadkill Review, Comstock Review, Confrontation, Delaware Poetry Review, Gargoyle, HEArt Online Journal, Innisfree Poetry Journal, MiPOesias, Moon City Review, Naugatuck River Review, Poet Lore, POETRY, Potomac Review, Public Pool, Rogue Agent, Scoundrel Time, Sojourners, Sweet: A Literary Confection, Tidal Basin Review, Tikkun, urbancode magazine, The Volta, Vox Populi, WORDPEACE, Word Soup.

"Gas" was written in response to the poem, "Recipe from the Abbasid," by Philip Metres, for his online series, *Sand Opera Lenten Journey*, 2016. "Yemenis Question U.S. Drone Strategy" is a found poem, written for *Before & After: Poets Respond to Shakespeare*, a project at the Folger Shakespeare Library curated by Teri Cross Davis. "After Poetry and Photographs in an Anacostia Gallery" was written for a series on hope curated by Joseph Ross at *The Basin Blog*, the blog of the *Tidal Basin Review*. "Drinking as a Political Act" and "In Guantanamo" also appeared in *Truth to Power: Writers Respond to the Rhetoric of Hate and Fear.*

"The Blueberry Seasons" was featured in The Poetry Moment outside the New Deal Café in Greenbelt, MD, and as part of "Nourish the Body, Nourish the Soul," a project of Rich Michelson, Poet Laureate of Northampton, MA, 2013. "For Dangerfield Newby, Freedman" and "Governor Bradford Watches the Indians *Fall Into Lamentable Condition*, 1633" also appeared on the site, *Poets for Living Waters*. "Flag of No Walls" also appeared (as

"The Flag of Touch") in *Poetry of Resistance: Voices for Social Justice*. "Hot Priests" also appeared in the *Cape Gazette*.

People in my life who have loved, cajoled, sustained me — there aren't sufficient pages in a book to thank you. Some of you are dear friends, some are brilliant poets, some are part of the astonishing worldwide community of Split This Rock poet-activists, some have lent their big brains to these poems, some are family, some are all of the above. I tried making separate lists. But you, my people, refuse categorization. I am grateful. Here's a partial list; it will never be complete.

Elizabeth Acevedo, Abdul Ali, Lauren K. Alleyne, Shatha Almutawa, Francisco Aragón, Deb Azrael, Lina Bahn, Holly Bass, Jan Beatty, Angelique Been, Richard Blanco, Kit Bonson, Chuck Bookman, Laure-Anne Bosselaar, Derrick Weston Brown, the extended Browning-Ripley family, Richard Buchsbaum, Regie Cabico, Carmen Calatayud, Grace Cavalieri, John Cavanagh, Sunu Chandy, Peter Coan, Nandi Comer, Nathan Congdon, Mary Jane Curry, Kyle Dargan, Teri Ellen Cross Davis, Hayes Davis, Anna Carson DeWitt, celeste doaks, Charles Doolittle, Amy Dryansky, David Ebenbach, Kathy Engel, Martín Espada, Julie Enszer, Danielle Evennou, John Feffer, Yael Flusberg, Rhonda Gans, Jennifer Freeman, Leah Harris, Niki Herd, Tom Hertz and the entire Hertz-Werro family, John Hill, all the Hutts, Rachel Gartner, Aracelis Girmay, Joseph Green, Alicia Gregory, Ken Grossinger, Katherine Howell, Natalie E. Illum, Chelsea Iorlano, Esther Iverem, Reuben Jackson, Jennifer James, Fred Joiner, Camisha Jones, Carolyn Joyner, David Keplinger, Alan King, Micheline Klagsbrun, Gowri Koneswaran, Bob LaVallee, Sarah Lawson, Pages D. Matam, Mieke Meurs, E. Ethelbert Miller, Peter Montgomery, Eve Müller, Tom Mullins, Don Myers, Elli

Nagai-Rothe, David Neigus, Yvette Neisser, Melody Nixon, Emily Norton, Naomi Shihab Nye, Dori Ostermiller, Lydia Perry Weis, David Rabin, Katy Richey, Kim Roberts, Simone Roberts, Joseph Ross, Lucia & Mark Savage, Susan Scheid, Johnna Schmidt, Tim Seibles, Andy Shallal, Don Share, Danez Smith, Patricia Smith, David Stevens, Tom Stoddard, Sonya Renee Taylor, Venus Thrash, Tiana Trutna, Jonathan B. Tucker, Melissa Tuckey, Dan Vera, Christie Walser, Zev Weiser, Kathi Wolfe, and many more.

Love and joy to my sisters and brother Katie, Rachel, Preston Browning, my father, Preston M. Browning, Jr., beloved nieces and nephews Anouk, Dakota, Julien, Grace, Sam.

Praises to the DC Commission on the Arts & Humanities, Virginia Center for the Creative Arts, Adirondack Center for Writing, and the Creative Communities Initiative for space and support to write. Extra thanks to Esther Iverem for the stunning cover art and to Aracelis Girmay and Tim Seibles for their spectacular words. And to Bryan Borland, Seth Pennington, and everyone at Sibling Rivalry Press — you opened my heart. Thank you.

About the Poet

Sarah Browning is co-founder and Executive Director of Split This Rock: Poetry of Provocation & Witness and an Associate Fellow of the Institute for Policy Studies. Author of a previous collection, *Whiskey in the Garden of Eden* (The Word Works, 2007), and co-editor of *D.C. Poets Against the War: An Anthology* (Argonne House Press, 2004), she is the recipient of artist fellowships from the DC Commission on the Arts & Humanities, the Virginia Center for the Creative Arts, and the Adirondack Center for Writing, a Creative Communities Initiative grant, and the People Before Profits Poetry Prize. She has been guest editor or co-edited special issues of *Beltway Poetry Quarterly*, *The Delaware Poetry Review*, and *POETRY* magazine. Since 2006, Browning has co-hosted the Sunday Kind of Love poetry series at Busboys and Poets in Washington, DC. She is a columnist for Other Words and her essays have appeared in the *Utne Reader*, *Sojourners*, and elsewhere. Browning previously worked supporting socially engaged women artists with WomenArts and developing creative writing workshops with low-income women and youth with Amherst Writers & Artists. She has been a community organizer in Boston public housing and a grassroots political organizer on a host of issues.

About the Press

Sibling Rivalry Press is an independent press based in Little Rock, Arkansas. It is a sponsored project of Fractured Atlas, a nonprofit arts service organization. Contributions to support the operations of Sibling Rivalry Press are tax-deductible to the extent permitted by law, and your donations will directly assist in the publication of work that disturbs and enraptures. To contribute to the publication of more books like this one, please visit our website and click *donate*.

Sibling Rivalry Press gratefully acknowledges the following donors, without whom this book would not be possible:

TJ Acena	Randy Kitchens	Paul Romero
Kaveh Akbar	Jørgen Lien	Robert Siek
John-Michael Albert	Stein Ove Lien	Scott Siler
Kazim Ali	Sandy Longhorn	Alana Smoot Samuelson
Seth Eli Barlow	Ed Madden	Loria Taylor
Virginia Bell	Jessica Manack	Hugh Tipping
Ellie Black	Sam & Mark Manivong	Alex J. Tunney
Laure-Anne Bosselaar	Thomas March	Ray Warman & Dan Kiser
Dustin Brookshire	Telly McGaha & Justin Brown	Ben Westlie
Alessandro Brusa	Donnelle McGee	Valerie Wetlaufer
Jessie Carty	David Meischen	Nicholas Wong
Philip F. Clark	Ron Mohring	Anonymous (18)
Morell E. Mullins	Laura Mullen	
Jonathan Forrest	Eric Nguyen	
Hal Gonzlaes	David A. Nilsen	
Diane Greene	Joseph Osmundson	
Brock Guthrie	Tina Parker	
Chris Herrmann	Brody Parrish Craig	
JP Howard	Patrick Pink	
Shane Khosropour	Dennis Rhodes	

www.ingramcontent.com/pod-product-compliance
Lightning Source LLC
LaVergne TN
LVHW041342080426
835512LV00006B/581